Boericke & Tafel

The Poultry Doctor

including the homeopathic treatment and care of chickens, turkeys, geese,

ducks and singing birds, also a materia medica of the chief remedies

Boericke & Tafel

The Poultry Doctor
including the homeopathic treatment and care of chickens, turkeys, geese, ducks and singing birds, also a materia medica of the chief remedies

ISBN/EAN: 9783337287306

Printed in Europe, USA, Canada, Australia, Japan

Cover: Foto ©Andreas Hilbeck / pixelio.de

More available books at **www.hansebooks.com**

THE

POULTRY DOCTOR

INCLUDING

THE HOMŒOPATHIC TREATMENT AND CARE OF

CHICKENS, TURKEYS, GEESE, DUCKS AND SINGING BIRDS.

ALSO

A MATERIA MEDICA OF THE CHIEF REMEDIES.

PHILADELPHIA:

BOERICKE & TAFEL.

1891.

PREFACE.

In actual money value, the products of poultry raising, including eggs, surpasses that of many ambitious
industries and is surpassed by few, if any, in the world,
be they agricultural or manufacturing. Notwithstand-
ing the great aggregate value of poultry, but little at-
tention has been paid to the medical treatment of the
ills of fowls, which are many, and what little they have
received has too often been of such a nature that they
would have been better without it. This, however, is
not surprising, for as long as men are ignorant of, or
deny the truth of, homœopathy, the great and only *law*
of cure, so long will they be incapable of formulating
any system of medicine applicable to all diseases,
whether of man, beast or fowl. Homœopathy offers to
poultry raisers a system of medicine for their fowls
which is exceedingly efficacious, involves little labor
and trifling expense. That system will be found de-
tailed in this book. What imperfections may be found,
must not be charged to homœopathy, but to imperfect

knowledge of the diseases of fowls. If *symptoms* can be clearly described, homœopathy will *surely* supply the remedy.

To Mr. P. H. Jacobs, of Hammonton, N. J., the well-known editor of the *Poultry Keeper*, and an extensive breeder of fine poultry, thanks are due for assistance rendered in classifying and accurately describing many of the diseases treated in this book.

CONTENTS.

" By similar things disease is produced, and by similar things administered to the sick they are healed of their diseases."—*Hippocrates.*

PART I.

HOMŒOPATHY AND ITS METHODS.

Similia Similibus Curantur.

IT has been said with truth that all subjects which arouse men, and cause them to divide into great contending parties, sooner or later crystallize into a word, or a terse apothegm, which contains a great truth. For a century homœopathy has excited keen interest and been fiercely fought. Its scope is as wide as disease and the cure thereof, yet is all crystallized in *Similia Similibus Curantur*. Like Cures Like. As with all great truths a child may comprehend, and a wise man study it a lifetime, and then realize that the unexplored fields are vast and the possibilities in them, for the welfare of man and beast, almost limitless. Homœopathy's work will cease only when disease no longer haunts the earth.

Illustrations.

"Like Cures Like," not the Same cures the Same—mark well the difference.   Perhaps the plainest illustration of this great natural Law—for Homœopathy is as much a Law as Gravitation—may be found in the well-known cure for a frosted ear, namely, rubbing it with a handful of snow.   Snow is not frost, but very much *like* it.   Like Cures Like.

Cinchona, or as it is known in homœopathy, **China,** if taken in large doses will produce, not chills and fever, but symptoms almost their exact counterpart; it will also cause excessive weakness, resembling that caused by loss of blood.   **China** relieves both these symptoms.

Arnica, if taken in strong doses, will cause a sore and bruised sensation, and, as all know, when externally applied will cure bruises and concussions; and, furthermore, as all do *not* know, it will relieve the bad effects from a concussion, blow, or fall; still better if taken in small doses, inwardly as well as applied outwardly.

Aconite will cause, among many other symptoms, that feverish condition which all experience at the beginning of a bad cold, and **Aconite** taken at once will cure almost any cold.   Let these few illustrations suffice, though the list might be extended to enormous length. Like Cures Like: therein lies the entire secret of medicine. Skill in application is obtained by the study of the symptoms of the sick man or beast and of the *Materia Medica.*

Materia Medica.

A concise *Materia Medica* of the remedies prescribed in this book will be found on its last pages, and a study of this part is recommended to all who would be successful in treating the ailments of their fowls. This *Materia Medica* is a record of the symptoms produced by the drug taken in excessive doses by men in a state of health.

The classification of diseases is, at best, but mere generalization. Take, for instance, "colds;" a dozen people may come together, each suffering from a "cold," yet the *symptoms* of no two of them be exactly alike. So with the diseases of fowls described in this book ; each one is named as well as may be, and the best known remedy prescribed, and it may be administered, as a rule, with great profit in the saving of the lives of poultry, yet an intelligent study of the *symptoms* of the affected fowls, and comparison of them with those of the different medicines, will greatly aid in the work.

Administration of Remedies.

The easiest way of administering the medicine is to dissolve two or three dozen pellets in a clean dish of pure water, and let the fowls drink it at will. If the disease is of an epidemic nature, like Roup or Cholera, it is well to let them all at it, for, given the correct remedy, it will cure the sick and prevent those still apparently well from developing the disease.

Another method and a good one, in view of the fact that chickens are nearly always ready to eat, is to dissolve the medicine in pure water and mix the water with corn-meal or moist food, and feed it to the flock, or the individual fowl, as the case may be. Another method is to moisten a bit of white bread in the medicated water, by which means a few fowls may be treated without the trouble of separating them from the flock. They can be driven aside and fed.

As a rule, where the ailment is confined to one, or a few, of the fowls, it is better to keep them apart from the others, where they can be treated with more care. The pellets can be given dry also, which is an excellent method, if practicable. Homœopathic medicines may also be had in liquid form, in which case from five to ten drops in water constitute a dose. Many people prefer them in liquid form.

After two days, if there is no marked improvement, select some other remedy; the chances are that the indicated one has not been chosen, for the true homœopathic remedy acts very quickly on fowls and animals —quicker, indeed, than on mankind—as fowls and animals do not injure their constitutions by unnatural living. When there is a marked improvement, discontinue the medicine, and do not resume it unless there are signs of a relapse. Too much medicine has been the bane of man and beast.

How to Keep Homœopathic Medicines.

Keep them well corked. Do not let the vials stand around open. Keep the vials in a box, in some place about the house where they are not exposed to undue influences of any sort. After the pellets are taken from the vial, do not put any of them back again. Keep them protected from the sun-light.

How to Procure Homœopathic Medicines.

Tha best way, of course, is to go to a homœopathic pharmacy and buy them; if this is not convenient, send twenty-five cents for each remedy wanted, to the address of some well-known homœopathic pharmacy, with the name of the remedy plainly written—*printed*, if you doubt the legibility of your penmanship—and a good sized vial will be mailed, postpaid, and securely packed. If there is a homœopathic physician in the neighborhood, he will no doubt be glad to sell you the required remedy.

Homœopathic medicines may also be obtained from some druggists; but in such cases it must be insisted on that the vials bear the labels of a homœopathic pharmacy—they are all sealed with a metallic capsule when put up for druggists' trade, and have the firm's name preparing them blown on the vial. There is good reason for this caution. The two schools work under different pharmacopœias, and the average druggist knows little or nothing of the preparation and dynamization of homœopathic medicines. Another, and a very urgent, reason for this caution is that homœopathy deals with very active poisons which, by the process of preparation, are rendered harmless for injury, unless taken in *oft-repeated* and long-continued doses, while still retaining all their curative powers. This leads us to the subject of

Dynamization or Potentiation.

It is, unfortunately, a common error to suppose that homœopathy means small doses and nothing more.

Homœopathy—Like Cures Like—says nothing about the size of the dose. In the early days, large doses were given until it was noticed that there were " aggravations"—drug symptoms—before cure, though the cure followed. This led to a reduction of the size of the dose. In doing this the drugs were minutely subdivided, and then the wonderful discovery was made that small doses reduced to atoms while mingled with milk sugar or alcohol were far more potent for cure than when administered in a cruder state. They had been *potentized, i.e.,* made more powerful in disease, and, at the same time, rendered comparatively harmless for evil if taken by mistake, by means of the small dose. That this theory of potentiation is correct can easily be demonstrated by the fact that men have swallowed leaden bullets or shot and experienced no bad results, while every one knows that if the same quantity of lead, reduced to the finest powder, were to be swallowed, the most terrible consequences would ensue.

The Truth of Homœopathy.

The crucial test of every scheme of medicine is its result with the sick. In this respect homœopathy leads all competitors ; indeed, truly viewed, it has no competitors, for it is the great Natural Law of Cure, while

others are but man's experiments, ever shifting and
changing; taken up as wonders and then dropped as
useless. Pleuro-pneumonia in cattle is pronounced incurable by the dominant school, and the government
orders all the afflicted animals to be slaughtered, yet
homœopathy could save nearly every case, as has been
repeatedly demonstrated. Homœopaths have secured
many a fine bargain in horses, buying an animal, pronounced incurable by some old school veterinarian, and
curing him. The large horse-car companies in almost
every city have adopted homœopathic treatment.

We will close this branch of our subject by giving
the statistics of an epidemic of comparatively recent
date, to illustrate the differences between the two schools.
During the epidemic of yellow fever in the southern
States in 1878, the allopaths treated 96,187 cases, of
which 12,296 died; a death rate of 23.5. At the same
time the homœopathic practitioners treated 3914 cases
of the same disease, of which 261 died; a death rate of
6.6. In many of the southern States, by means of
unjust medical legislation, the allopaths have obtained
sole control, and they refuse to permit homœopaths to
practice. This accounts for the great disparity in the
numbers treated.

Medical legislation is a subject of vital importance to

the people, and they should see to it that no medical monopoly is granted. These laws, on their face, look very plausible, and claim to "protect the public," but even "quacks" could not have made a worse showing than that of the "regular" profession in the epidemic of 1878.

PART II.

SOME PRACTICAL HINTS.

THERE are a good many books on the general management of poultry. All of them contain some good matter and, also, much that is impractical and even useless, or worse. The most of them seem to take it for granted that every poultry raiser can devote a great deal of his time to the care of his fowls. They seem to be constantly addressing men who make poultry raising their sole business; whereas the number who do so compared with those to whom it is merely an incidental part of farm life, are as one to many thousands. It is to the larger class that this book is addressed, and our aim is to give here only such hints as may be easily acted upon. Those who follow poultry raising as a business, perhaps know more on the subject of the care of fowls than the book writers do, but many of them have much to learn in the treatment of the diseases of poultry.

Where poultry is allowed the run of the farm during the warm months the question of feeding is settled by the fowls themselves, but when winter comes they must be fed. When this time arrives those fows will thrive best that are given some *variety* in their food. Do not give them the same stuff day after day, but vary it if possible. Hens, like horses and men, are the better for a change of diet. Especially give them at times something green, throw in a head of cabbage and let them revel on it.

Another point that involves little trouble and no expense is to see that they are provided with clean water often renewed. Water that is unfit for a human being is not good for hens. A little common sense comes into good play here; the horse, cow, dog and hen eat and drink what they can get; if their food and drink does not suit them, no complaint is heard; they do not grumble or raise a disturbance as man does, but follow St. Paul's advice, and eat what is set before them. Their only protest against unfit food and drink is to sicken and die without a complaint. Did you never notice how eagerly a caged bird hops over and drinks when his water cup is filled? He evidently appreciates it as much as a man would who was given a glass of fresh water in place of some that had stood in his bedroom

2

over night. The same rule applies to all animals. In this matter, "directions" are not needed, but only a little common sense flavored with humanity.

Another parallel between man and hen : In the human family the mortality is greatest in infancy, and so it is in the hen family. Some mortality in both families is unavoidable, but much in both may be avoided by a little extra care. To be trite, prevention is better than cure. At the very dawn of its existence the young chick mostly needs warmth. If this warmth be combined with moisture the death-rate must rise; therefore Dame Partlett and her brood should be caged in some place protected from the wet ground and the rain, and the dame will provide the warmth. Furthermore, keep the cage clean. It is not much trouble, and it pays. Who has not seen a cage with its floor an inch thick with dirt and the whole sodden by having the pan of water spilled over it! Better let them run than be caged with such a mess. Another point—but it involves a little care; who has not seen a hen with her chicks trailed out behind her making their way through the wet grass of early morning! Each little fuzzy beggar is draggled up to his neck and looks, and is, no doubt, thoroughly miserable. The hen ought to have better sense, but she hasn't. If she and her brood could be kept confined until the grass were dry it would be better for the little ones.

Mr. Judd, in his book on poultry, makes some good points on the feeding of very young chickens. He very strenuously objects to the common Indian, or corn, meal dough that constitutes the sole food of so many young chicks. It is tumbled out to them, and if not all eaten allowed to stand until it is eaten ; it usually sours, the chicks, perforce, must eat it, as nothing else is provided, and then they sicken and die. Mr. Judd says : " For the first morning meal I give all my young stock boiled potatoes mashed up fine and mixed with an equal quantity of Indian meal and shorts. I find nothing so good and acceptable as this food, and I use only small and unmarketable potatoes ; they prove more profitable than anything else I can employ." This food is followed with *fine* cracked corn. But whatever is fed to the young chicks the gist of the matter is, do not feed them anything that has turned stale or sour. There is death in such a mess, and it is economy to throw it away.

We know that wild and domestic animals require salt, and from this it would seem right to assume that fowls require it too, though the want appears not so pressing in their case. It is said that fowls who eat their own feathers cease to do so when given salt. How salt should be given them is an open question. In salting food the danger is in excess. Too much salt for man or beast will result in sickness, and very bad sickness at that. Salt in large quantities seems to be fatal to poultry, but may safely be used to season the food.

What the wash-bowl or bath-tub is to man, a dust pile, dust-box or dust in some shape is to the hen. It doesn't look like a very cleanly way of performing the toilet, but it is her way, and chicken raisers will do well to see that the dust-bath is provided in some shape. It is supposed that this bath is a means of ridding the feathers of lice ; mixing a little insect powder with the dust will aid in this. Some authorities prefer fine sand to dust. If the hens will use it, sand seems better than dust. Fine ashes are also recommended.

Let the chickens get at corn-stalks in winter, occasionally ; it helps in the assimilation of food. Scalded clover hay, however, is better and furnishes an excellent substitute for green food, but it must be finely chopped.

Onions chopped up are eagerly eaten by fowls, and are excellent for their health, especially if their eyes are not in good condition.

Dried tobacco leaves in the nest of a setting hen keeps

it clear of vermin, and adds greatly to her comfort and that of her young when hatched.

Chickens fatten best when given a full feed just before going to roost, and the first thing in the morning.

A dry floor may be obtained by digging out the earth and replacing it a foot deep with sand.

A hen's laying capacity reaches its highest point in her second year, and then begins to decline.

In reserving cocks for breeding purposes, keep those that are the most active and vigorous.

There should be at least one cock to eight hens; one drake to four or five ducks; one gobbler to ten turkey hens, and one gander to two geese.

Do not let fowls inbreed too long or the result will be loss of eggs and deterioration of the flock.

Where poultry is allowed the run of a farm there is no danger of over-feeding, but there is with yarded poultry which gets no exercise; these especially require variety.

One great secret of successful turkey raising is regular feeding during the fall and winter in one place. This makes them tame and prevents that tendency to wander off in summer and breed, which is innate in the turkey.

During " fly-time " a flock of turkeys will easily live on insects, such as grasshoppers, etc., and are, therefore, valuable in two senses, but it is not well to raise them unless they can have a wide range. When confined they easily " eat their heads off."

Ducks do not eat more, if fed regularly, than other fowls of their size, and will be marketable at four months age, and the large breeds may be made to attain five pounds when ten or twelve weeks old; neither do they require a pond or stream, but may be raised where chickens can be raised; they require plenty of good drinking water and some pasturage. A stream or pond of water, of course, is an advantage.

Poultry does well under woman's care, and is very profitable. A lady writes that in one year, after having furnished her own table with nearly a hundred fowls, and with all the eggs needed, she was enabled to sell considerably over one hundred dollars worth of eggs and fowls. The cash outlay bringing in this return was about twenty-five dollars.

Chickens ought to have a house for winter, even if it consists merely of a few boards nailed together, a mere shanty, lined with paper. The cost of such a shed will be slight, but it will pay.

Barren, sandy patches about the farm can be profitably employed as poultry ranges. Fowls are freer from disease on a sandy soil and will fertilize it to a considerable extent.

If possible, don't have any green, slimy pools of water about. They are bad for man and hen.

Give fowls and animals all the light possible. Light and pure air are health givers. Darkness and disease are allies.

Plough or spade the poultry yard at times; it keeps the earth clean and tends to promote the health of the fowls.

"Chicken powders" and advertised compounds promise all sorts of wonder working. Little or nothing is known of them. If "stimulating," remember that stimulants act on animals as on men—feel good for a while and then not. Good food is all a fowl needs in health and the indicated homœopathic remedy in disease.

Whether charcoal, asafœtida, Cayenne pepper, etc., are good to "promote health," is a very wide, open question. Some believe in them—we don't.

PART III.

THE TREATMENT OF DISEASES.

Preliminary Remarks.

THERE are no colleges established for the study of the diseases of poultry, and there are no graduated poultry physicians, and, outside of homœopathy, there is little, if any, belief in the efficacy of medicine in treating the ills of feathered creation. Indeed, an eminent authority on poultry rather drearily remarks: "It is almost useless, and rarely ever worth while, to treat sick poultry." This is true if no treatment, but what, for the sake of distinction, may be termed allopathic, is known, but it is *not* true if homœopathy be employed. In the latter case, the labor involved is next to nothing, the expense very slight, while the treatment is highly effective, as has been demonstrated in thousands of cases, and this most markedly so in epidemic diseases which carry off entire flocks.

One of the greatest difficulties to overcome in writ-

ing a work on the ills of poultry is in *naming* the
the diseases. A careful comparison of the few treatises
published heretofore on the subject, reveals the fact that
a disease that in one place bears one name, takes on
another in another part of the country. Fortunately,
however, this fact, which would prove so disastrous
under other systems of medicine, is but of slight
moment in homœopathy, for it treats diseases, not according to their names, but according to their *symptoms*, and a little knowledge of the action of the various
remedies will enable any one to treat a sick fowl intel-
ligently and quite independently of the *name* of the
disease.

Homœopathic remedies may be classified into groups
or families; the individuals of which differ yet have
many traits in common. In the following pages the
remedy chiefly indicated by the disease is first given,
but it may not be the correct one in all cases, and the
others named afterwards may then be administered in
their order.

Those having homœopathic " family medicine cases "
(and every family living in the country should have
one) may use the medicines in them. The same medicine applies equally to fowls or human beings; there is
no difference in the preparation of medicines for " veter-

inary" purposes from those used in treating human ailments.

The number found following the name of the remedy on the vial, as "**Arsenicum 6,**" refers to the *potency.* Minerals, like arsenic, are usually sold in the sixth potency and others in the third.

Apoplexy.

This disease, as with men, is caused by over-feeding, and occurs with all classes of poultry when in a very fat condition. The bird afflicted staggers and falls ; its breath comes heavy and short, and somewhat resembles snoring ; eyes protruding, staring and generally highly bloodshot. It is frequent to find apoplectic birds dead under the roost, when they were apparently in excellent health. Open the bird's mouth and give it half a dozen pellets of **Belladonna.** · Other remedies are **Aconite, Nux vomica** and **Pulsatilla. Nux vomica** may even be better than **Aconite.**

Asthma.

Canary and other singing birds are often troubled with asthma. The breathing is easily heard, and especially after the exertion of flying. **Corallium rubrum,** a half dozen pellets dissolved in the water-cup effects a speedy cure. **Spongia** is also indicated; also **Ipecac,** in case of too much flesh, and **Bryonia** in asthmatic panting of old age. A little plantain seed is said to aid recovery in obstinate cases. This disease is often mistaken for roup.

Bone-wen.

This disease has always been deemed incurable, but where homœopathy is employed a cure is possible, if not probable. Isolate the afflicted fowl and dissolve six pellets of **Hepar sulphuris** in its water dish every day for a week, unless marked improvement sets in sooner. If at the end of the week no change is noticeable change the medicine to **Silicea,** same dose each day. Other remedies are **Nitric acid, Calcarea carb.** and **Sulphur.** When changing remedy it may be well to give the last named for one day before following with the new remedy.

Black-rot.

In this disease the comb turns a blackish color, legs may swell and emaciation accompanies. Bad food and unhealthy surroundings seem to be the cause ; remedy these and give **Thuja.** The true remedy for this disease is problematical, depending on the cause of the disease. **Nux vomica** may be called for and **Podophyllum,** if the seat of the derangement be the stomach or liver respectively.

Broken Bones.

When bones are broken in fowls one can readily see at a glance what is the trouble if it be a leg bone. With other bones a break can be detected by examination only, when a swelling will appear over the broken bone which is evidently painful to the touch. These usually heal themselves if the fowl is kept quiet. A compound fracture is beyond the skill of most people, but a simple break is not. Bring the broken parts gently but firmly together, bind with linen bandages and hold in place by a couple of appropriate sized splints. Moisten the linen frequently with a lotion of one part tincture of **Symphytum** mixed with five parts water. How long the treatment is to continue must depend on the condition of the fracture, and that, the one having charge of the case alone, can decide. After the operation give the patient one dose of **Aconite**, say three pellets in the mouth and at the expiration of a week put six pellets of **Hepar Sulph.** in the water for one day only.

Bumble Foot.

This is caused by the foot getting hurt in some way, bruised, or possibly a sliver run in it. It is often the

result of high roosts, the feet being injured when jumping therefrom, especially if the bird is heavy. The hurt
part swells, becomes inflamed, pus forms, which in time
grows hard and cheesy-like. The treatment is to wash
the hurt clean, see that no foreign substance remains in
it, then bathe in a lotion of one part **Calendula** tincture
to five parts water, and bind up the foot as neatly as
possible and keep bandage wet with the lotion ; or, in
place of binding the foot anoint it with **Calendula
cerate,** or lotion, and keep the fowl on clean straw. After
operation give **Hepar sulph.** if hurt has not " gathered ; "
if it has, give **Silicea.** During the few days necessary
for healing, the fowl should be kept caged in a clean
place.

Chicken-pox.

Some writers designate this disease " small-pox." It
is known by blotches on the comb and neck and pustules under the wings and feathers generally, while the
fowls seem weak and melancholy. Homœopathically
treated it is not dangerous. The disease is contagious,
and the sick should be separated from the well, though
if the flock is pretty generally attacked let the treatment
extend to all. The treatment consists in dissolving from
one to three dozen pellets of **Arsenicum,** according as a
few or many are afflicted, in the drinking water. Con-

tinue for three days. If no improvement is noticed
change the remedy to **Rhus tox**. Renew the medicine
each day, using fresh pure water. Also indicated, **Belladonna** with hot fever. **Silicea** if pustules " break."

Chip.

" Chip " or " chipping " derives its name from the
peculiar cry or sound made by the bird, and it is prin-
cipally attributed to lack of warmth, or exposure to
cold draughts (sometimes from the top ventilator). It is
confined chiefly, if not entirely, to young chickens, and is
caused by wet weather, the light down on the little fel-
lows getting wet and having no chance to dry. It is
very fatal if not taken in time. Chickens afflicted with
" chip " seek refuge in solitary places where they are detected by the regular and plaintive cry, and generally remain there until they die ; they exhibit tenderness on
being touched, and perceptible fever, although they
tremble violently as though cold. If possible they
should be given dry shelter and warmth. A number of
remedies are indicated in this disease, so many, indeed,
that it is difficult to decide which to give the preference.
It is best, perhaps, to begin with **Veratrum**, as that
remedy " has external chill with internal heat," a most
distressing feeling. A dozen or more pellets dissolved

in the drinking water, or, if they will not drink, dip a little white bread in the water and let them eat it if they will. Among the other remedies are **Arsenicum, Aconite, Dulcamara** and **Colchicum**, the last named being preferred by some authorities. Give the selected remedy twenty hours trial, and if there is no improvement, change to one of the others named.

Cholera.

It was frequently observed at the times and places when cholera was epidemic among human beings that chickens, turkeys, geese and farmyard fowls generally, became in many instances similarly affected. At the present day the word "cholera" is applied to an epidemic which while varying somewhat in different parts of the country is always accompanied by a violent diarrhœa, and is very fatal. Some of the characteristics of this disease are : Sad looks, lost appetite, weakness, staggering, thirst, hanging heads; in more advanced stages a tough mucus trickled from the bills, which hang so low as to touch the ground, the comb becomes shrunken and of a bluish color, while the diarrhœa is violent and almost liquid, yellowish or greenish, frothy ; as the end approaches the eyes close. Being an epidemic it is well to treat the entire flock, though if the sick can

be isolated so much the better. European writers highly
commend **Veratrum alb.**, both as curative and as pre-
venting the spread of the disease. Dissolve anywhere
from two dozen pellets to half the vial (according to size
of flock) in water given the fowls to drink, or take part
of the water and moisten their food with it. **Arsenicum**
is also quite as valuable in cholera; the symptoms of
both remedies bear great resemblance, **Arsenicum** being
indicated in the second stage where there is great prostration.

Arsenicum iod. (iodide of arsenic) has by clinical
experience proved effective, as the following experience
reported by Dr. Robert Boocock in the *North American
Journal of Homœopathy* shows : " **Chicken Cholera.**—
I can fully endorse the curative power of *Iodide of
Arsenic* in certain forms of humid asthma, having been
successful in a few cases. I want to speak of this medicine as a means of curing the summer complaints we
often meet during the hot weather. Two years ago I
lost almost all my chickens by chicken cholera. Last
summer a new lot of hens and chickens began to die off
by the same disease, and I thought it a good chance to
try **Arsenicum iod. 3.** I mixed about two pounds of meal
with two drachms of the remedy, and left the mixture in
the chicken house for them to take at will. It cured

every case. I had a good lot of it left to throw away. In severe cases of cholera infantum it promptly cured when all our usual remedies failed."

Parched corn, or parched cracked corn, almost to coffee-color, is an excellent food for flocks during cholera season—not exclusively but as a part of the food.

Constipation.

This complaint may afflict any of the feathered creatures and is easily recognized. The fowl is restless and cannot evacuate, although making frequent effort; if any stool does pass, it is small in quantity and very hard and dry. The cause of the trouble lies in long-continued feeding on dry and heating food, such as barley, oats, rye, hemp seed, etc., together with impure water and lack of any green food. It occurs chiefly among fowls confined in coops or narrow yards. It may be also the result of cold. **Nux vomica,** half a dozen pellets to the fowl, dissolved in its drinking water, or mixed with food, will usually remove the complaint if caused by the food. **Bryonia,** if resulting from cold or other causes. A change of food, or, rather, giving the fowl something green in addition, is also required. But the medicine is necessary to give thorough relief, for the mere giving of green stuff may only result in altering the character of the disease without eradicating it. **Opium** is another remedy for constipation, indicated when there is *no urging.*

Contusions.

If a fowl gets a severe blow or hurt in which no bones are broken, bathe the hurt with a lotion of one part **Arnica** tincture to twenty parts water, and put a few drops of the water in the fowl's mouth. **Arnica** should never be applied to man or beast undiluted. It acts better when diluted.

Consumption.

This disease in fowls seems to be pretty much the same as in human beings—bad heredity or resulting from a cold which is allowed to run on without care. There is a cough, the fowl seems to eat well, yet grows emaciated. "Incurable" is the general verdict, a verdict which no believer in homœopathy should admit to be true, even though he cannot, with his present knowledge, name the proper remedy. This consumption of the lungs must be distinguished from the "consumption" spoken of under "Marasmus." In both there is a wasting away, but the seat of the trouble is different. This is a disease that is sometimes classed in the

Roup family of ailments. Remedies can but be suggested : **Hepar sulph.** and **Spongia** on alternate days may cure, or **Calcarea carb.**, given alone.

Core.

Core consists of the formation of an excrescence in the gullet or alvine passage. It is generally brownish-yellow in color, but varies in this respect. **Arsenicum, Mercurius** and **Silicea** are the three remedies mostly indicated. The disease is difficult to detect owing to its situation.

Coryza or Catarrh.

This is not at all an uncommon complaint, and it causes considerable losses, being also one of the difficulties sometimes classed as *Roup*. With pigeons it often occurs during moulting, and is contagious, and sometimes plays havoc in the pigeon roost. Pigeons suffering from coryza keep their bills open, and a yellow-looking mucus may be seen in the nostrils ; the mouth also looks yellow. If the disease is noticed in time, remove the infected bird, but if a number are affected, it is better to treat the whole lot. **Mercurius viv.** will generally cure ; a dozen pellets dissolved in clean drinking water, or the water used in mixing soft food. Continue until cured, or if no improvement is noticeable in a few days, change the remedy to **Acidum sulph.**, in same way.

In hens, coryza is generally caused by catching cold in continuous wet weather, or by very sudden changes in the weather. It is characterized by an increased discharge from the nostrils and sneezing. At times it is epidemic. **Arsenicum** will usually give prompt relief. A dozen or more pellets dissolved in the drinking water, or in half a tumbler of water, and then this mixed with meal or used to moisten bread. **Arsenicum** failing, give **Mercurius viv.** Should the discharge thicken and the eyes seem affected, give, in same manner, **Euphrasia.** Should the coryza occur from dry, cold winds, **Aconite** is the remedy.

Coryza is particularly dangerous with turkeys. The turkey seems uneasy, trembles, an acrid, slimy discharge comes from the nostrils and the eyes grow dim. If possible, separate the sick turkey from the well ones, and administer to it **Acidum sulph.** or **Mercurius viv.** As with pigeons, the disease seems to attack the turkeys during moulting time.

H. Fisher, V. S. of Berlin, reports the complete and satisfactory cure of a valuable parrot who was suffering from a bad coryza or catarrh. The bird ate little and breathed with a rasping sound, and was evidently suffering from a bad cold. **Dulcamara** and **Hepar sulph.**, in alternation twice a day soon removed the trouble.

Hepar sulphur is the best remedy when there has been partial relief from other remedies but not complete cure.

Gelsemium is an excellent remedy for catarrh incurred during *warm, moist, relaxing weather.*

Catarrh or coryza in fowls must be distinguished from roup, as a common bad "cold" is distinguished from croup or diphtheria in human beings. The discharge from the nostrils of fowls in catarrh is thinner and not offensive, and is accompanied with sneezing and coughing, while in roup the discharge is thick and very offensive. Cold, catarrh, coryza, roup and pip are all more or less related to each other.

Cough.

Turkeys are often afflicted with a cough resulting from small red worms in the windpipe. The disease seems to be the same as "gapes" in chickens, and calls for the same medication, *i.e.,* **Dulcamara** and **Drosera,** in alternation with **Sulphur,** to complete the cure. For external treatment, see "gapes."

Diarrhœa and Dysentery.

While resembling, in some respects, cholera, these

ailments are essentially quite different. The discharges
are copious, sometimes bloody, the feathers about the
anus befouled and the fowl out of condition, though not
so greatly prostrated as in cholera. "Scouring" is another name for the trouble. All fowls are subject to
it. The cause is damp, cold weather; cold on the
stomach; brooding in damp, cold stables; feeding on
noxious berries or plants; eating too many worms; over-
feeding, also want of lime or gravel necessary to the
digestion of hens. **Ipecac.** is the chief remedy, a dozen
or more pellets, owing to number to be treated, in
water, or mixed, after being dissolved, with the food.
If directly traceable to bad food, remove the cause and
give **Arsenicum. Chamomilla,** also, has cured. Hens
sometimes have a whitish discharge which oozes out,
fouling their feathers; for this, give **Carbo veg.**

Among geese there is a disease known sometimes as
"white dysentery." The geese lose appetite, become
weak and breathe hurriedly; the evacuations are very
soft and of a chalky color, and finally liquid. The
body or flesh assumes a bluish color and the bird then
dies. The disease runs its course in three or four days.
Bad food, filth, browsing in bogs and swamps, are the
general causes. With geese so afflicted it is best to
cage them up in a dry place on clean straw (keep it

clean) and feed good food. The first day give them **Aconite**, two or three dozen pellets in the drinking water. The next day give **Arsenicum** (wash the drinking vessel thoroughly on changing medicines, or get a new one). **Mercurius viv.** and **Chamomilla** are also useful.

There is also a species of bloody flux or inflammation of the bowels, which attacks turkeys and hens when closely confined, fed on bad food and given foul drinking water. The abdominal walls get thin and transparent, and there is a sinking in the region of the anus; a bloody, mucus-like diarrhœa accompanied with rapid emaciation. **Mercurius cor.**, in clean, pure water, is the best remedy. **Ipecac.**, also, is useful.

There is a disease among geese and ducks originating from the same causes as the preceding, which, in some respects, resembles it, yet which post-mortem examination shows to be inflammation of the spleen. Geese, when attacked, begin to shriek, put their heads to the ground, fall over on their backs, go into convulsions and die. Where the disease has progressed so far, there is no help for the sick. But the remainder of the flock may be cooped up or confined, given good food and pure water, in which **Arsenicum**, as a preventative, has been dissolved ; give this remedy for three days, changing water

every day. One German authority, Traeger, prefers
Nitric acidum dissolved in water, and the water used
to moisten the meal or other food given. The amount
of each remedy should be in proportion to the number
treated—from one dozen to three dozen or more pellets.

Dysentery carries off a great many parrots, especially the young ones. A few doses of **Mercurius
cor.** will speedily cure. It may be stated, that, in
general, **Mercurius cor.** is the remedy for the worst
cases of dysentery, especially " painful bloody discharges."

Diseases of the Eye.

The cause of sore eyes in hens is uncertain. Some
breeders attribute it to the weather and others to over-
heating, dust and sundry other causes. Perhaps all
have something to do with it. The eyes are watery,
ulcerated, with discharge of offensive-looking liquid,
and, in time, pus sores are formed. The sick fowls are
also very apt to fall rapidly away. If there is reason
to suppose the complaint is caused by the weather,
which is more frequently the case, give **Aconite** in the
beginning; but for bad cases or those well advanced,
Euphrasia or **Sulphur** are better, the latter, if there is
pus formation. **Apis** is indicated when the eyes are

inflamed, sore and swollen, but not complicated with colds or other ailment.

Distemper.

" Hen distemper " is a plague occurring in hot, dry weather, and is commonly attributed to atmospheric conditions. The hens lose their bright, cheery look, have a puffed face of deep scarlet color ; crouch about in corners and die one after the other. The disease is contagious, and if not too much spread through the flock, the sick ones should be isolated. Examination reveals the fact that the skin around the anus is inflamed and red, with black spots occurring. The best remedy is **Nux vomica,** which has proved successful.

Students of poultry books will, no doubt, experience some confusion on reading the foregoing, for some of their books connect hen distemper and cholera, while others associate it with roup. Which are we to believe? they may ask. The reply is, ignore the *name* and attend to the *symptoms*. If the foregoing symptoms are met, administer **Nux vomica.**

Dizziness.

Dizziness seems to be the best term, or, at least, the most descriptive. In geese it is sometimes known as " staggers " and sometimes denominated by the syno-

nym, " Vertigo." Geese and ducks are mostly afflicted
with it, but hens and turkeys are not exempt. The
signs are, drooping wings, stretched-out neck, or twisted
about in all sort of ways, the body is often shaken, and
turned around and around until the bird falls over and
dies. Fat, or over-fed fowls are mostly subject to it.
The cause is variously attributed to a rush of blood to
the head, to worms in the nostrils or ears, and to the
results of blows on the head. It will be seen from this
that the ailment is difficult to treat, or rather to deter-
mine which of the three causes should be treated. The
rush of blood calls for **Belladonna** and plenty of cool,
fresh water for drinking. If caused by a blow, **Aconite,** followed by **Belladonna.** If from worms, give
Cina, or a little turpentine or kerosene in the nostrils
may remove the trouble; should they be in the ears,
the case is difficult; to fill the ears with sweet oil or
milk is about the only safe course. As a rule, however, dizziness is but a symptom of some malady.

Dropsy.

This disease only, as a rule, attacks old and fat hens
who have ceased laying. The malady is manifested by
a swelled abdomen and ruffled plumage. The fat seems
turning to water. If any one wishes to treat dropsy,

Apocynum cannab. or **Apis** are the best remedies; the former, if there is heaviness and general sluggishness; the latter, if there are evidences of the disease on the skin. It is better, however, to destroy a bird so afflicted.

Epilepsy.

Pigeons are sometimes attacked by a disease called, perhaps improperly, epilepsy. It manifests itself by the contortions or unnatural workings of the muscles of the throat, and if touched the birds seem to be in pain. The disease oftener attacks the female than the male. Its cause is unknown. **Belladonna** covers the symptoms best.

Feathering.

Every one knows that babies during dentition, or teething, often get very sick. Something analogous occurs with young fowls when their down begins to be replaced with feathers; that is their " teething " period. To the best of our knowledge this complaint has never been classified and named. We have called it "feathering," because the word, if homely, is certainly descriptive. Most poultry raisers have at some time carried a lot of young chicks or turkeys safely through infancy only to have them, when feathers begin to sprout, perversely die. This will happen even where the care, food and housing is of the best. What is the matter? The owner asks the question of his editor, and that gentlemen—doesn't answer satisfactorily.

When young fowls of this age begin to droop and die they should be carefully examined to make sure that lice are not the cause. If no lice be found there is a plain call for medicine. There are no incurable diseases given if treated in time and the proper homœopathic remedy selected. The condition described is so vague that no remedy can be with certainty prescribed, but the probabilities are that a helpful one will be found among the three following : **Calcarea carb., Chamomilla** or **Hepar sulph.** The conditions distinguishing these remedies must necessarily be vague. In general, **Calcarea carb.** when there seems to be arrested growth, **Chamomilla,** when there is foul evacuation, and **Hepar** when the chick looks scrofulous or, so to say, mangy. Even a fourth remedy may be added, and a good one— **Aconite,** when there is *restlessness,* "crying," and a general feverish condition. Administer the remedy, a dozen or more pellets, in the water cup or food of the fowls; in the latter case dissolve in water and mix thoroughly.

As already stated, this is merely suggestive. It is an analogy between the teething of babes and the growing of feathers. But the losses are so heavy at this period of fowls' lives that a remedy is needed, and we believe can be found in the foregoing.

Gapes.

Every poultry raiser knows what the malady known as "gapes" is. It chiefly attacks young fowls before their feathers have grown, and is manifested by a more or less constant "gaping" of the mouth, or, more properly, a gasping for breath. It is due to the presence of a small red worm in the windpipe. Whether this worm is bred without the chick, or is a spontaneous generation resulting from physical causes, is an open question. In all probability the disease is due to constitutional defects which may be removed by the proper remedy. In a disease of this sort the remedy must be prescribed somewhat empirically, as there are no parallels between this disease and the provings. German homœopathic writers assert that **Drosera** and **Dulcamara** given on alternate days will cure the disease. Among suggested remedies may be named **Ignatia, Lachesis** and **China.**

If it should ever be discovered that the worms are bred in the stomach and ascend thence, as is most probably the case, then the remedy unquestionably would be **Cina,** or the active principle of that remedy **Santonine,**

and we would advise putting the young chicks on **Cina**
for a few days, when, if there is no improvement, resort
may be had to one of the other remedies.

Among the more popular external treatments may be
mentioned the twisting of a horse-hair into a fine loop,
running it down the bird's windpipe and pulling the
worms out, also taking a small feather, stripping it, ex-
cept at the point, dipping it in turpentine or kerosene
and running it down the throat, after having bent the
feathered part over so that it will go down with the
grain of the feathers. There are many other treatments
recommended by various authorities, such as flour of
sulphur, crude camphor, turpentine, etc., but the trouble
with them all is that there is always danger of killing
the chick along with the worm.

Gout.

This disease commonly known as "gout" would seem
to be more akin to "rheumatism." Hens and turkeys
are mostly liable to it, and it also attacks ducks and
geese when they sleep on damp floors. The cause is
taking cold, or exposure to cold and wet, which settles
in the legs and feet; damp pavements and filth also
combine to produce it. The legs and feet swell and become stiff, and the fowls walk with difficulty, their gait

suggesting that of a rheumatic person. The first
requisite in the treatment is a dry place for the fowls,
and if their legs could be rubbed down with mutton
tallow, so much the better. **Bryonia** or **Rhus tox.** will
cure, however, without the tallow. **Dulcamara** is also a
good remedy. Turkeys seem more subject to this disease
than other fowls.

Hernia.

Hens laying unusually large eggs are at times troubled
with hernia. The larger species of fowls are more apt
to be troubled by it than the smaller. The intestine
through which the egg passes protrudes abnormally, and
does not recede when the hen leaves the nest.

To attempt to treat this ailment externally involves
rather a disagreeable proceeding, as it must be repeated
a number of times. The treatment consists in washing
the protruding part in lukewarm water or milk, anoint-
ing it with linseed or sweet oil and gently forcing it back
into the body. This repeated several times will cure
the trouble. This treatment should be accompanied
each time with a dose of **Aconite** to allay any fever.
The internal remedy is **Pulsatilla** or **Nux vomica,**
i.e., when the external treatment just mentioned is not
resorted to.

Hoarseness.

Caged singing birds are subject to attacks of hoarseness; in other words they "catch cold" from being exposed to draughts, the same as men do. There are a number of remedies for this ill, and they are easily administered by dissolving half a dozen pellets of the chosen one in the bird's water cup. If the bird sneezes and is evidently just taking cold, **Aconite** is the remedy, but if it is plainly hoarse, tries to sing but has little voice, and that rough in sound, give **Causticum** or **Hepar sulph.** If there is great hoarseness, watery eyes, yet occasionally the voice breaks out clear, give **Pulsatilla.**

Humid or Black Disease.

Humid, "black" or "sweating" disease sometimes attacks hens who are setting and remain too long on the nest at a stretch, especially if the nest be too damp and cold. Under the wings the featherless parts will be found blackish looking and clammy. Medicine can hardly do any good in such cases. The best cure is to make the hen air herself more. Also, look carefully for lice, both for the little red mites and the large gray lice. Some writers recommend washing the under part of the wing with tepid water. But this process may excite

the hen so much that it may " break up " her setting.
Carbo. veg. will aid, or **Sulphur.**

Indigestion—Dyspepsia.

This complaint is evidenced by unhealthy evacuations
of partly or wholly undigested food, diminished or total
loss of appetite, and sometimes retching, vomiting and
a "tucked up" crop. It is supposed to be caused by
over eating. Confine the bird by itself, let it fast a little
and give it half a dozen pellets of **Nux vomica** dissolved
in its water cup. If this does not correct the trouble,
change the remedy to **Pulsatilla,** especially if there has
been retching or vomiting. **China** and **Carbo veg.** are
also good remedies.

Itch.

Itch is a contagious disease. Some care must be used
not to confound it with lice or chicken-pox. Examin-
ing the fowl will enable one to distinguish the one from
the other. A hen with the itch is constantly scratching
and biting herself, her feathers become droopy and fall
out. Examination reveals the fact that her body is
covered with small pimples, larger on the back than
elsewhere. Give **Sulphur** in the water for three days,
and then follow with **Staphisagria** until the cure is

4

complete. Keep the fowl, or fowls, caged during the treatment.

Kriebel.

We have given this malady the German name for want of an English one. It is, we believe, unknown to American poultry raisers, though, probably, their fowls have suffered from it and they did not know its cause or confounded it with some other ailment. The cause of it is smut and ergot, a peculiar excrescence found growing on grain. That found on ears of corn is called smut, and on rye and wheat is called ergot, in some seasons when the weather has been hot and moist, though it is found to a certain extent in all seasons on the corn. Chickens fed on corn containing much smut develop the following symptoms: Dizziness, staggering gait, lack-lustre feathers, leanness, lay few eggs and refuse to hatch; sometimes they fall on their sides and draw their claws convulsively together when they attempt to arise; the final symptom is a decay of the comb and feet, and then death follows. It will be seen from this that no matter how carefully fowls are attended they cannot escape "kriebel" if fed on corn or grain containing much smut or ergot; many a well-kept hennery may have been decimated from this cause, much to the puzzlement of its proprietor. The cure, of course, is plain—remove the cause. The health of the flock will be regained more rapidly by giving it three or four dozen pellets of **Solanum nig.** every day in the drinking water.

Lice.

The dangerous louse to poultry is the large "grayback," who works on the head, neck and vents, is hard to find as it lurks close down on the skin at the roots of the feathers, and is so blood-thirsty that one or two are enough to kill a young chick. These lice are with chickens all the time, but especially during July and August. Search for them on the *head, neck and throat.*

Bowel disease in summer is a sign of lice; the sleepy disease, in which the chicks are sleepy or drowsy, is a sign; refusal to eat; puny looking body, and slow growth; sudden deaths; gradual wasting away; constant crying; loss of feathers on the head; and other symptoms that appear surprising or remarkable. Even in the *cleanest* of houses, when not a sign of lice can be seen, look on the chicks for the *large lice.* Not only on chicks but the large body lice are *nearly always* on adults. A chick will never get lousy unless the old fowls are near, and that is the reason why brooder chicks grow faster than those under hens. The large lice will kill ducks suddenly. They kill nearly all the young turkeys that die. Whenever you notice a sick fowl dusting itself *look for lice.*

There are as many remedies for these pests as there are " cures for warts " among school boys, and yet the lice flourish. Here are some of them :

Wash the fowl with a decoction of absinthium (worm-wood).

Oil of fennel dropped on the head or neck will drive away lice.

Clean the coop or hen-house thoroughly and white-wash it equally as thoroughly. Rub the roosts with a mixture of kerosene oil and lard ; if this is kept up for a time the vermin will disappear.

. Fumigate the hen-house with a pan of live coals and a handful of sulphur. (Also be very careful you do not set it on fire by so doing.)

Apply kerosene freely to perches and wherever the lice may find refuge.

Put a little, a very little, kerosene on the fowls' neck-feathers, and this will drive away the lice from the fowls. Be careful not to put on too much, as it is irritating. A good ointment for lice is made by mixing a cup of lard with a teaspoonful of kerosene.

To clear a house of fleas, mites, ticks, lice and such parasites, clean it, wash it with hot lime wash, sprinkle the floor with a solution of carbolic acid, and grease the roosts with a mixture of one pound of lard, one pint of raw linseed oil, quarter of a pint of kerosene and a quarter of a pound of sulphur.

For lice among pigeons, clean the house, or cote, thoroughly, and sprinkle it with camphorated water, and supply the birds with plenty of bathing water.

Green twigs of alder put into the coop, or house, and removed next day, will be found covered with the vermin.

If handfuls of wild thyme be thrown in the coop and about the hen-house, lice will rarely trouble the fowls.

To clear singing birds of lice, keep the cage clean, immerse it in scalding water, and let the bird bathe frequently. If lice are on the bird, take a piece of flannel and put some turpentine on it. Catch the bird and wrap him up in the flannel as closely as you can, without hurting him, leaving only his head exposed. Hold him for a few minutes and then release him, and the flannel will be found covered with lice, or some lice, at any rate. Fire or scalding water is then the best treatment for the lice after being caught.

Among the numerous parasitic pests of fowls, is one which we may call "red mites." They are noticed as being in countless myriads on the walls and roosts.

Another class of mites, parasitical, are found under scales, on the combs, and on the legs below the feathers. If unmolested, the comb grows thicker at the base, darker, and furrowed. The feathers of the head and neck fall off. The disease is infectious, and when a fowl is attacked, it should be caged apart from the flock. The treatment must be external. The parts may be painted with kerosene or washed with carbolic soap. Another good treatment is to wash the affected parts and then anoint them with sulphur cerate, which may be obtained at any homœopathic house. Another good ointment, and one that can be home-made, is two parts of sweet oil or lard to one part kerosene. "Scabby or scaly legs" in poultry are due, perhaps entirely, to these parasitical pests, and they may be entirely removed by a little care—washing the leg and rubbing it with the kerosene ointment, or a *very* little pure kerosene. A dozen pellets of **Sulphur**, in the water-cup of the fowl under treatment, renewed every day, will aid in the cure enabling the fowl to regain a healthy skin and comb much sooner than without it.

One ounce oil of cedar mixed with a pint of other oil and put on the neck, back, etc., of chickens is said to clear the lice away. Only a few drops should be used, as grease is repugnant to fowls.

For young chicks: two parts glycerine, one part carbolic acid, the two mixed with five times their bulk in water. Apply freely to sprouting feathers.

In conclusion, and in the words of an experienced poultryman, "lice means *work.*"

Liver Complaint.

It is rather difficult to detect this complaint until the fowl is killed, when the liver will be observed to have an unnatural color and a certain rotten or cheesy look. When alive, the fowl has, if it may be so expressed, a jaundiced and bilious look, with alternate attacks of diarrhœa and costiveness. **Podophyllum** will cure the trouble. Many cases of this difficulty are caused by the use of copperas solutions in the drinkng water, by inexperienced poultrymen, known as Douglass mixtures.

Marasmus.

Marasmus, or "consumption," as it is sometimes called, though neither designation seems to be quite correct, is that disease in which the glands, secreting an oily fluid among the tail feathers, becomes stopped. When this occurs the fowls cease scratching, sit about morose, biting often at the root of the tail feathers, become constipated, grow lean and die. The external treatment is to reopen the glands, if possible, or to anoint the part with oil—sweet oil being best.

Such treatment, while palliative, is not really curative, for it is fair to assume that the disease is not due to external accidents. The homœopathic remedy for the complaint is **Hepar sulph.** Isolate the fowl, if possible, and put a dozen pellets of the remedy in her water-cup.

Moulting.

Properly speaking, this is not a disease but a normal process through which the fowls pass without difficulty. Should it happen that the process is slow and the fowl seems in a generally, dry, arrested condition, give it **Calcarea carb.** If there is a raw corroding fluid among the feathers, give **Natrum muriaticum.** If fever, **Aconite.** Oily foods, such as sunflower-seeds, linseed-meal, etc., are beneficial during moulting.

Pip.

A disease that affects the tongue and mouth of the fowl, and is evidenced by a tough, scaly growth on the tongue, and is often the result of dryness of the tongue due to the clogging of the nostrils, which cause the fowls to breathe through the mouth. The term "pip" is now seldom used. The "regular" treatment is to remove the scale or skin from the tongue with a knife, and at the same time put a little chlorate of potash into the mouth. But this heroic treatment is now generally abandoned, and is both troublesome and, far too often, totally ineffective. The homœopathic treatment, on the other hand, involves no more trouble than mixing the pellets in the water of the fowls and arranging that they drink it.

The disease seems really to be a species of sore throat or diphtheria, brought on by sudden change in the . weather, or catching cold in some way. The hens are listless, sit with open mouth, nostrils are clogged, comb looks unhealthy, and the crop is mostly empty, probably on account of the difficulty in swallowing. As with roup, to which it is akin, **Spongia** meets most cases, though **Mercurius viv.** is also indicated. In many instances one dose of the former remedy completely cures. If, after several days, no improvement sets in, change to **Mercurius viv.** If the complaint is very prevalent, give the remedy to the entire flock in their water or food; if confined to a few, isolate them. Dose: from a dozen up to four or five dozen pellets, owing to size of flock. In this, as in all other diseases, there is not the slightest danger in giving too many

pellets, for the curative virtue lies in the *similia* of the
dose and not in its " strength."

Roup.

Under this heading is grouped, too often, the whole
series of catarrhal affections. If Webster's Unabridged
is opened and " Roup " looked up, the inquirer is referred to " Roop;" turning to that word he is again
referred to " Croup," and that really is " Roup."
Dunglison's Medical Dictionary also gives the same
derivation. The difference between croup and diph- .
theria, in brief, and, what closer study would probably
reveal to be analogous, roup and pip, is, that in roup
the mucus remains slimy and stringy, while in pip it
hardens and forms the "scale." Be that as it may,
roup is the bane of chicken-raisers and of chickens.

The disease is characterized by a foul breath, offensive discharges from the nostrils, inflamed and swollen
head, sore eyes, and a cankerous-looking throat and
mouth.

The homœopathic remedy for roup is **Spongia**, and
if homœopathy had done nothing else for poultry
breeders than to give them this remedy, it would merit
their lasting gratitude. Of its efficacy there can be no
doubt. **Spongia** is the sovereign remedy for croup in

children, as countless thousands could testify, and it is the same in croup, or roup, of fowls. That this theory is correct is confirmed by experience wherever the remedy has been administered to fowls. Breeders, who heretofore had lost fifties and hundreds from roup, find that their loss under **Spongia** diminished to next to nothing.

In administering the remedy, all that is required is to dissolve from a dozen to four dozen pellets in clean water, and put the water, the usual quantity apportioned to the fowls, in a clean vessel, where they will drink it. Continue until the disease has disappeared, which will be in a very short time.

The disease sometimes called " Rattle " in geese seems to be nothing but a species of Roup, and **Spongia** is the remedy for it.

Among other homœopathic remedies for Roup may be mentioned **Hepar sulph., Aconite, Arsenicum** and **Tartar emetic.** But these will hardly be called for often.

Before closing this subject it may not be amiss to quote the following testimony from a correspondent of *The Poultry Keeper*, a well-known journal :

" I don't know but it will be in place to say something more of the *Spongia*. When I last wrote I was trying it on a rooster that had the Roup for six months. For a wonder it cured him up. Of course it would be impossible

to do this in every case. You know I wrote you several times about losing
my young chicks with the Roup. Well, I lost three lots—150 in all. I kept
on trying, and, after using the *Spongia*, I have only lost a few, and will have
winter frys instead of spring frys."

Another correspondent writes as follows:

" I am now prepared to state unconditionally that *Spongia* did it; circum-
stances as more favorable weather, and my own rather costly experience
of last year may have had something to do with it ; but the facts are that,
from July, 1889, when the roup invaded my flocks, until February, 1890,
when by dint of the 'survival of the fittest,' health was again in a measure
restored in my poultry house, my chickens have yielded me very little in-
come, and less pleasure ; handling and dosing, isolating and fumigating,
until I was almost suffocated and entirely disgusted.   One-third of my
entire flock succumbed.   Fact is also that although not a believer in
homœopathic remedies, I used *Spongia* this year on the strength of the
Poultry Keeper's recommendation, as soon as the dreadful disease showed
itself, about the middle of August, and the last and most satisfactory fact is
that my hens and chickens never were in better health than they are now,
and have been since the beginning of September ; only a single chicken
out of 150 having died of the disease.   Certainly, single examples do not
prove a case, but if the experience of many others, which will not be slow
to come in, should show that in *Spongia* we have a simple and effective
remedy against as terrible a scourge as roup, the poultry fraternity may
well congratulate itself and thank the *Poultry Keeper*."

The foregoing was written by a gentleman in Wisconsin. Here is a bit of experience from one, a citizen of New York :

"I had about twenty cases of roup in my flock this fall.   I tried turpentine, glycerine and carbolic acid, in proper proportions, without effecting a
single cure, and also used chloralum and several other remedies without
any good effect.   I commenced *Spongia* about a week ago, and part of them
are now well, and there is a very marked improvement in the rest of the
cases."

Another poultryman writes :

"Since you sent me *Spongia* for a roup recipe I have given it a thorough trial, and find it strikes the very vital parts and *does the work.* I have tried a number of recipes, and they all proved a failure, and with the same symptoms, and every condition, the *Spongia* has *cured in every instance,* and for your advice in the matter I am under many obligations. I have quite a good place here and expect to raise a large number of chickens the coming season."

And still another :

"At the time I commenced using the *Spongia* I had fifteen or twenty cases of roup, and new ones coming down every day. They soon commenced to show signs of improvement, and are *all now entirely well. Spongia did the business."*

Later issues of this journal contained abundant confirmatory evidence of the inestimable value of **Spongia** in Roup ; one number contained letters from twenty different correspondents from all parts of the country testifying to the curative powers of **Spongia.**

It may not be out of place to emphasize again the necessity of getting *Homœopathic* **Spongia** to obtain these results. We once read an Allopathic professor's account of how **Spongia** is prepared and can affirm that if any one administered the remedy prepared as he directed no results would be obtained.

Swelled Crop.

Caused by eating too much or from something that prevents the food from passing out of the crop, as the

passage from the crop to the gizzard may be clogged
with long dry grass, old rags, or other substances. The
hen ruffles her feathers, throws her head back and her
crop feels packed ready to burst. Fasting and gentle
manipulation generally cures. **Nux vomica** or **Arsenicum** will aid in giving relief. Some breeders as a last
resort cut the crop a little with a very sharp knife, with-
draw the food and sew up the wound with a silk thread.
In the latter case anoint the cut with **Calendula cerate**,
or, if that is not at hand, with **Arnica** and water.

Swelled Head.

From some cause not clear, the heads of hens will
often swell greatly and be very hot. Exposure to
draughts of air, however, is a fruitful cause of both
swelled heads and swollen eyes. **Spongia** has given
relief in many cases but **Belladonna** is the indicated
remedy for this trouble ; **Bryonia** also will relieve.

Thrush (Aphthæ).

Consists of small vesicles or white specks on the mem-
brane of mouth, tongue, etc. There are several remedies
for this condition of sore mouth or Stomatitis ; among
them may be named in their order: **Nitric acid** if there
is a general yellowish appearance; **Mercurius viv.** if

red, spongy, bleeding ; **Staphisagria** if pale, white and readily bleeding ; and **Thuja** if there appears to be a fungus-like growth.

Tumors, Excrescences.

Domestic fowls are sometimes attacked with Tumors, which anyone will recognize at a glance. Isolate the fowl and dissolve a dozen pellets of **Arsenicum** each day in its water cup if it is supposed the Tumor is a natural growth, or, if caused by injury, **Hepar sulph.** Cauliflower-like excrescences or seedy warty growths require **Thuja.**

Vesicles.

Small Vesicles, or pimples about the size of a pin-head, and pearl-like, will sometimes be found on the neck, comb and wattles of fowls. They hunt sunny places, droop their wings and grow lean. On the seventh day the Vesicles ripen and improvement sets in or the fowl dies. Isolate the affected ones. **Nitric acid** is the best remedy ; dissolve in the water cup a dozen or more pellets each day until cured.

Warts.

Warts do not trouble fowls often. The best general prescription for them is **Thuja.** Occasionally there is met with in pigeons and other fowls, warty, cancerous

or ulcerous growths in the mouth and throat. It is
difficult to cure, but **Arsenicum** will in many cases
relieve. For what is known as " Wart Skin " (not
Chicken-pox) give **Calcarea carb.**

White Comb.

This disease is said by German authorities to be a
vegetable parasite or fungus, which attacks fowls sometimes. The combs become covered with what looks
like a whitish dust, the feathers grow scrawny and the
fowl dies. The complaint seems to be contagious, and
the fowls affected should be isolated. The treatment
recommended by the German poultry men is **Sulphur**
for a day or two in the drinking water, followed by
Staphisagria, which is the main remedy.

Something which somewhat resembles this complaint
will be found under the heading " Lice."

Worms.

When any fowl is known by observation to be
affected with worms, **Cina,** or the active principle of
that remedy, **Santonine,** is the remedy. Continue until
good health is restored. Raw flesh is generally the
cause of worms, but not always.

PART IV.

A BRIEF MATERIA MEDICA

OF THE

CHIEF REMEDIES PRESCRIBED IN THIS BOOK.

THIS Materia Medica, condensed from the standard homœopathic text-books, gives some of the more prominent indications calling for the remedy named in human beings; the same indication demands the same remedy, whether it occurs in man, beast or fowl ; thus readers will not only be enabled to obtain a clearer knowledge of the remedy their fowls require, but at times to select a remedy for their own ills. It must not be inferred that *all* the symptoms, under a remedy, must be present in order to call for it. A few of them, or even one, will be relieved by the remedy if truly indicated.

Aconitum.—*Restlessness.* Anxiety. Headache as if the brain were moved or raised. Eyes staring, red, inflamed. *For inflammation resulting from foreign substances in the eyes.* Violent sneezing, feverish, thirsty with coryza. *For beginnings "of colds."* Toothache in sound teeth, or *neuralgia*, from

5

exposure to cold, dry winds. Dry burning throat. *For beginning of pleurisy or pneumonia.* Spitting of bright, frothy
blood. Pressure as of a weight in the pit of the stomach. Urine
hot, painful, red. Milk fever. Teething, with hot inflamed
gums. Laryngitis, with inflammatory fever. Dry, hacking
cough. Hot breath. Oppression of the chest when moving
fast. Pulse full and hard in fevers. Great irritation of the
nervous system. Skin red, dry and burning; sweating when
covered and attacks of chilliness. Sleeplessness of old age.
General indications are dry fever. heat, and especially restlessness. Aconite is very useful in the first stages of a large number
of ailments.

Apis.—Inflammatory affections with *great swelling*, almost
like dropsy. The pain is of a biting, stinging, burning character,
like that arising from the sting of a bee. A great indication
for the selection of this remedy is the *want of thirst* in spite of
fever and inflammation. The same holds good in dropsical
affections. Sore throat with *stinging* pain when swallowing.
Incipient diphtheria. Erysipelas. An extremely valuable
remedy in a great variety of diseases of the eye, inflammatory.

Apocynum Cannabinum.—Heaviness of the head
evenings. *Hydrocephalus.* Great thirst, but water disagrees.
Dropsy. Acute inflammatory dropsy. Excretions of urine and
sweat greatly diminished. Dropsy and dropsical conditions.

Arnica Montana.—*Externally.* A lotion of one part
tincture to ten of water, to be applied to all injuries from falls,
blows, concussions and sprains. *Internally* (in pellets), for all
heavy blows or concussions. Bladder affections from mechanical
injuries. Pleurisy from mechanical injuries. Rheumatism of

laborers. Palpitation and "strain" of the heart after violent exertion. "Clergymen's sore throat." Bruised feeling. Great physical fatigue. Ill effects from blows or heavy exertion generally. Neuralgia following injuries. Nose bleed with "blackish" blood.

Arsenicum Album. — Headache, motion aggravates. Chronic eruptions, with pustules on the head. Violent burning in the eyes. Discharges of cadaverous odor from the ears. Watery discharge causing burning and smarting in the nostrils. Cancerous ulcers on the face. Eruptions, sores and ulcers on mouth or lips. Thirst, drinks often but little at a time. Frequent vomiting. Vomiting immediately after eating. Heat and burning in the pit of the stomach. Diarrhœa after chilling the stomach by food or drink. *Ill effects of cold water or ice cream.* Hœmorrhages from bowels, dark and offensive. *Asiatic cholera with watery discharges.* Sudden catarrh threatening suffocation at night. Difficult breathing. Tightness of chest. Agonizing heart pains. Trembling limbs; violent starting while falling asleep. Very rapid sinking of strength. Dreams full of care, sorrow and fear. Eruptions, pimples, carbuncles, cancers, *lupus. Bad effects from tobacco chewing, quinine or alcohol.* Bites of animals. Sudden and extreme debility, burning pains and bad eruptions. Hœmorrhoids, with burning, like fire.

Arsenicum Jodatum (Iodatum).—Enlarged scrofulous glands. Blood poisoning with debilitating sweats. Eruptions in syphilitic patients. Last stages of diphtheria and croup, putrefaction. Diarrhœas, dark, mushy stools.

Belladonna.—Delirium. Blood mounts to the head.

Jumping, violent, throbbing headache, eyes feel as if starting from their sockets. Headache from heat of the sun. Face swollen and hot. Violent thirst and desires sour drinks. *Scarlet fever.* Attacks of coughing, as if from dust. *Erysipelas. Bad effects from smoking tobacco. Peritonitis.* Suits full-blooded people. Congestion of blood. Red, inflamed swellings, red, feverish states.

Bryonia.—Headache beginning in the morning and increasing, as though the head would burst, till evening : *worse on motion.* Hot, soft puffiness of face. Coryza, with greenish discharge from the nose. *Bitter taste.* Angry, disagreeable temper. Soreness in pit of stomach when coughing. *Biliousness.* Desire to breathe deeply, but cannot on account of pain in the chest. *Pleurisy.* Pains in the joints. *Rheumatism.* Great aggravation of suffering from heat. *Constipation : stools hard, dark brown or black, dry, as if burnt.* Lumbago. Profuse, offensive sweat. Yellow skin. In general, bilious complaints and all complaints worse on motion. Catarrh with dryness. Dry mouth and throat. *Lumbago.*

Calcarea Carbonica.—Scrofulous ophthalmias. Hair dry, falling out, dandruff, and generally *scabby and unhealthy.* Sore, ulcerated nostrils. *Ozena.* Face pale, bloated, old and wrinkled looking. *Difficult teething.* Cough dry : expectoration salty. Chronic dyspepsia. *Felons.* Feet cold, damp, bunions. Takes cold easily. Epilepsy ; marasmus. Cracking of joints, as if dry. Headache in school children. Scrofulous inflammation of the ear. Skin dry, shrivelled. *Ringworms.* For rickety and scrofulous people or unhealthily large children ; big headed. Enlargement of the liver, with jaundice ; liver sore. Chronic dyspepsia, with aversion to *warm* food or drink. White swelling of knee-joint. Inflammation of hip-joint. *Chronic* form of intermittent fever. Many cases of goitre.

Camphora.—Sudden and extreme prostration. Face pale, livid, cold. Cold sweat. *Cholera. Cholera morbus. Sickness from tobacco.* Tongue cold. Mouth cold. *Summer complaint.* Body cold. Strangury. Influenza when patient feels cold and chilly. Hands cold, bluish. Great prostration, Impotence. Chill, with shivering and shaking; chattering teeth. Unhealthy coldness. Cholera, cramps, cold prostrations. (N.B.—The remedy used should be homœopathic camphora, and not the crude drug from the "camphor bottle.")

Carbo Vegetabilis.—Ailments from eating fat meats, pork, etc., or in waterbrash, sour risings, great flatulency with constant eructations. Spasms in the stomach with burning and aching pains. Ailments after abuse of mercury, as offensive breath, bleeding of the gums, canker in the mouth. Useful in all kinds of foul-smelling discharges, even from ulcers. *Bad effects from drinking ice water, such as colic.* Senile gangrene, humid leg. Corrosive leucorrhœa.

Causticum.—Ailments resulting from suppressed eruptions like *measles, scarlatina,* etc. Loss of voice. Paralytic conditions, sciatica. Weakness of the neck of the bladder, children wetting the bed. Acid dyspepsia. Horny warts.

Chamomilla.—Child cries, quiet only when carried; whining, restless; wants things, and when offered pushes them away; peevish, nothing pleases, one cheek red while the other is pale. Eructation sour, inclination to vomit. Convulsions of children. Stool green, watery, or like chopped eggs, with colic. For children during teething and for infantile colic, earache. A valuable remedy for uterine hæmorrhages.

Cina.—Child does not want to be touched ; cannot bear you to come near it ; uneasy and distressed. Child picks at its nose. Grinds its teeth when asleep. Unnatural hunger. The chief remedy for worms in children. (*Santonine* cures worms if *Cina* fails.)

Cinchona (China).—Heaviness in the head, fainting, temporary loss of sight, ringing in the ears ; cold surface. After hæmorrhage. Vertigo, after loss of animal fluids. Headache worse in the open air, better from hard pressure, Habitual nosebleed. Flatulency. Heartburn. Hectic fever, frequent night sweats, diarrhœa, pallor, sleepless, nervous. After exhausting disease or loss of animal fluid. Chills and fever, especially in swarthy persons. For all losses of animal fluids. Rapid emaciation, with indigestion, voracious appetite, undigested stools and copious night sweats. Ringing in the ears.

Colchicum.—Great thirst but no appetite, smell of food disgusting. Intense neuralgic headache, with ineffectual efforts to sneeze. Stomach icy cold, colic distension. Breathing asthmatic. Rheumatic pains in elbow, wrist, finger-joints. Œdematous swelling and coldness in legs and feet. Tingling in toes like after being frosted. Smell of cooking nauseates. Wants things, but when brought they nauseate. Useful with asthmatic, gouty, rheumatic people.

Corallium Rubrum is very serviceable in nervous coughs and whooping- cough, mostly during the spasmodic stage ; also, in Millar's asthma of children. Sensation as if cold air passed through the respiratory organs, when taking a long breath.

Drosera.— *Whooping-cough* in periodically returning paroxysms, with vomiting, the child feeling better during motion than during rest. Whooping-cough with hæmorrhage from the nose and mouth; nose-bleed, especially morning and evening, or when stooping. Cough *worse at night*, and made worse by singing, laughing, crying, smoking and drinking. Oppression of chest as if air could not be expired.

Dulcamara.—Dull headache, continuous. Aching in eyes when reading. Coryza worse after slightest exposure. Salivation. Menses suppressed by cold. *Rheumatic pleuritis and pleuro-pneumonia* with tough, difficult, discolored sputa. Erysipelas of feet. Pains in the joints after exposure to cold. Rending pain in side, upward. Tetter oozing a watery fluid, bleeds after scratching. Nettlerash with much itching; after scratching it burns; increases in warmth, better in cold. Fleshy warts. Useful, in general, in ailments *arising from cold, wet weather*, especially in phlegmatic, scrofulous, torpid, people; catarrhal troubles always *worse in cold, wet weather*, with free secretion of mucus; lameness in small of back after getting wet.

Euphrasia.—Eyes with swollen agglutinated lids. Thick yellow discharge from the eyes. Stitching pressure in the eyes. Sensation as of sand in the eyes. Opacity in the cornea. Catarrhal ophthalmia with lachrymation and mucous discharge. Profuse flow of acrid tears. Inflammation and ulceration of the margin of the lids. Profuse, bland, fluent coryza, with scalding tears and aversion to light. Cough, can scarcely get breath.

Attacks of heat during the day, with redness of face and cold hands. Has strong action on ailments of the eyes in connection with colds.

Gelsemium.—Complete loss of muscular power from want of nerve-tone. Paralysis. Cerebro-spinal-meningitis. Infantile remittent fever, and other fevers having a remittent character. Feverish conditions with great restlessness. Neuralgia with nervous twitchings. Prostration from night watching. Weakness of sight, double vision. Affections from prostration of hot weather. Hiccough if chronic. Writer's cramp. Especially useful for all " colds," or catarrhs, contracted in hot, moist weather. Catarrh.

Graphites.—Dirty crusts on the scalp. Every thing turns black before the eyes when stooping. Styes on lower lid; wens on the lids. Eruptions behind the ears; fissures; scabs. Dry scabs in the nose, with sore cracked, ulcerated nostrils; purulent, fœtid secretion. Scabs on the face, skin dry, beard falls out. Rotten odor from mouth and gums. *Tape worm. Fissuro ani.* Emissions without erections. Nocturnal emissions, flaccid (long-standing complaint). Hydrocele, left side. Leucorrhœal discharges in gushes. Hard scars. Abscess. Hard, dry respiration. Horny hands, cracked raw places, nails black and rough. Callous ulcers on the feet (*quarter crack in horses*). *Burning in old scars. Old scars from ulcers.* Will remove or lessen scars. For unhealthy, hard, dry, cracked, scabby skin and slow foul ulcerated conditions.

Hepar Sulphur.—Morning headache worse from every jar. Boils on head and neck. Falling out of hair, with sore pimples and bald blotches. Discharge of fœtid pus from the ear. Pain-

ful boils. Scurfy eruptions. Loose rattling cough. Croup.
Unhealthy skin, slight injuries suppurate. Ulcers discharge
bloody pus. Sweats day and night without relief, or first he
cannot sweat, then profusely. Promotes suppurative process as
in abscess, boils, sty, gumboils, "run-rounds" and whitlow; for
" ripe colds " and effects of abuse of mercury.

Ignatia Amara.—Useful in hysteric affections ; also con-
vulsive and spasmodic disorders, especially when occasioned by
grief ; great excitability of the nervous system ; pain from the
least touch ; headache as if a nail were driven into the head,
better from eating ; chronic nightly cough ; concussive spasmodic
cough, especially on walking. Pain and pressure in the throat
between the acts of deglutition, as if a ball were lodged there.
Sciatica recurring during cold weather. Sciatica in general.

Ipecacuanha.—Heat and throbbing in head, with red
cheeks. Loss of smell ; catarrh *with nausea*. *Nausea* constant
with all complaints. Vomiting, bile, dark-colored substance
with or without blood, sour fluid, *always with nausea*. Inde-
scribable sick feeling in the stomach. *Diarrhœa*, fermented,
greenish, slimy, bloody followed by straining. Diarrhœa from
unripe fruit. Urine scanty, dark red ; unsuccessful urging.
Profuse menstruation *with constant nausea*. Nausea with attend-
ing ills ; chiefly of mucous membranes and stomach.

Merc. Subl. Corr.—Ophthalmia with profuse discharge.
Inflammation of the bowels. Dysentery, if accompanied by
retention of urine ; stools of blood and mucus. Bloody micturi-
tion ; inflammation of the urethra with yellowish discharge.
Fever, with burning heat, cold sweat. Nightly bone-pains.
Bloody flux. In general similar to mercurius but more violent.

Mercurius Vivus.—Head feels as if in a vice or bound with a hoop, worse at night. Fœtid, sour-smelling oily sweat on the head. Purulent discharge, green from the ears. Coryza, nose red shining swollen, worse at night. Teeth loose, toothache from caries; gums painful, swollen, bleeding, *receding from the teeth*. Ozæna, offensive, sore bones. Erysipelatous inflammation of the throat, rawness, roughness, mouth full of saliva; tonsils dark red, ulcerous, but rarely diphtheritic. Constipation, stools tenacious or crumbling, violent straining, sometimes with blood. Cough, violent racking, worse at night as if head and chest would burst, short breath and sometimes bloody sputum. Scrofulous catarrh. Aching in the bones. Paralysis agitans. *Chronic* inflammation of the liver with jaundice. *Syphilitic conditions generally.* Venereal ulcers.

Natrum Mur.—Intermittent fever, chill beginning in the morning, backache. Profuse sweat having a sour smell. *Malarial poisoning.* Headache, as if bursting ; beating or stitches through neck and chest. Excessively sore, red eyelids. Heartburn always after eating. Constipation; difficult stool with fissures at the anus. Chronic catarrh of the ear. *Greasy skin.*

Nitric Acid.—Useful in inflammation and ulceration of the bones ; syphilis and sycosis ; tedious suppuration and glandular diseases ; sore throat, from syphilis on abuse of mercury ; pricking pains as from *splinters;* carious ulcers ; pain in old sores on change of the weather ; brown-red spots on the skin and boils. Is often required in secondary syphilis and mercurial ailments, small-pox. Pneumonia in old people. Bleeding warts. Bad freckles of the skin. (Resembles Mercurius in many respects.)

Nux Vomica.—Hypochondriac mood of persons of sedentary habits; of those who dissipate. Headache from drinking spirituous liquors; red blotched face or yellow and florid. Eyes burning and smarting. Toothache with swollen face. Taste ; bitter, sour, tongue heavily coated white, or yellow. Bad effects of coffee, alcoholic drinks and debauchery. Indigestion after abuse of drugs (too much allopathic or "patent" medicines). Sedentary habits, high living. Liver swollen, sensitive caused by debauchery or high living. Jaundice with constipation, from sedentary habits or abuse of alcohol. Alternate constipation and diarrhœa. Roughness and rawness in the chest. Nervous prostration from mental overwork.

Opium.—This remedy is frequently suitable to drunkards and old people, and to persons on whom other medicines are slow to act. Dream. Stupid sleeplessness; consequence of fright; trembling, jerking convulsions beginning with rigidity of the whole body, loud cries; epilepsy; tetanus; painters' paralysis; delirium tremens ; expectoration of frothy blood when coughing ; constipation from torpor of the bowels ; stupor occasioned by falls, blows, or other accidents. Valuable in apoplexy with stupor and cold extremities ; also in threatened apoplexy of drunkards.

Phosphorus.—Impending paralysis of brain and collapse; softening of the brain. Dandruff copious; hair comes out in bunches. Bad effects from excessive use of salt. After drinking as soon as water becomes warm it is thrown up. Jaundice with pneumonia or brain disease. *Sexual excitement, lascivious dreams, emissions and weakness.* Asthma with fear of suffocation ; loss of voice, rattling breathing, hoarseness with cough and rawness ; cough worse at night and changing from warm to cold. Broncho-pulmonary catarrh. Pneumonia, weight on chest. Typhoid pneumonia. Pleuritis. Tuberculosis in the tall, slender or rapidly growing. Great debility, frequent attacks of bronchitis. Clammy sweat. Blood boils. Open cancers bleeding easily. General tendency to fatty degeneration. Softening of the brain; brain always feels tired.

Podophyllum.—Excessive secretion of bile ; great irritabilty of the liver ; torpidity of the liver; jaundice ; chronic hepatis ; hyperæmia of liver. " *Bilious attacks.*" Prolapsus ani, with stool, even from least exertion, followed by stool or thick, transparent mucus, or mixed with blood. Piles with prolapsus ani and long standing diarrhœa. Bilious temperaments.

Pulsatilla.—Especially adapted to *female derangements,* children and to persons of mild, gentle dispositions, but valuable in many complaints of all persons. Headache from overloaded stomach, pastry, fat food., Rheumatic headache. *Deafness,* as if ears were stopped ; from cold; earache ; bland, nearly inoffensive discharge, Coryza, with loss of sense of taste and smell, or diminished. Loss of taste with catarrh, nothing tastes good. Thirstlessness. Eructations, tasting of food. Pressure on the pit of the stomach after eating ; colic from cold with diarrhœa ; from ices, fruits, pastry. Phthisis florida, suppurative stage ; chlorotic girls. Pain in chest, as if ulcerated. Catching pains in region of the heart, burning, palpitation. Stitches in small of back. Pain in small of the back, as from stooping long. *Pains that shift from place to place.* Hysteria. Fainting fits, pale face, shivering. *Epileptic convulsions from suppressed menses.* Tired, worn-out feeling. Flitting chilliness, now here, now there. Emaciation.

Acts especially with light-haired or blue-eyed, fair people. Old, painful chilblains.

Rhus Toxicodendron.—*Stiffness or lameness on first moving after rest;* better after exercise. Complaints from getting wet while over-heated. Erysipelas. Burning, drawing, tearing in face. Fissure of anus, with periodical, profuse, bleeding piles. Stiff neck, pain in shoulders and back, with stiffness, as from a sprain. Effects from getting wet or sleeping in damp, cold places. *Lumbago,* increased by cold. Sciatica. *Sprain from over-lifting. Rheumatism,* joints stiff or red, and shining. Eruptions, red, measly rash, itching, burning. Eczema, surface raw. Chilblains. Valuable for effects of strains on the muscles from lifting. Muscular rheumatism, without much fever or inflammation. Acne rosacea.

Silicea.—Violent periodic headache. Amblyopia of the eyes from abuse of stimulants. Coryza long lasting. Caries of the bones. Carious teeth. *Ailments caused by vaccination.* Lack of vital warmth ; scrofulous constitutions ; foot sweat; waterbrash with chilliness ; cough hollow, spasmodic; night sweats. Nails yellow, brittle. Cancer ; fistulous openings ; yellow, dirty, or wax-like skin. While **Hepar sulphur** tends to promote the suppurative (festering) process, bringing it out "to a head," **Silicea** tends to heal that already established. Abscess at roots of teeth.

Spongia Tosta.—Headache in back part of the head. *Membranous croup,* suffocating attacks, barking cough. Thick, offensive, viscous mucus. Laryngismus stridulus. Inflammation of the larynx, trachea and bronchia. Chronic cough, violent attacks, brought up small, hard tubercle. Asthma. Wheezing, laboring breath. Herpes.

Staphisagria.—Hypochondriacal, apathetic, weak memory, face sunken, weak legs, backache, prostration, resulting from abuse of sexual organs. Herpes, dry, with scabs. Ulcers in scurvy. Toothache from old decayed teeth. Certain deep coughs, not chronic. Chronic gout with nodosities.

Sulphur.—Affects the whole organism, rendering it susceptible to the action of other remedies, but more noticeably *acts on the skin ;* itching; freckles; yellow, brown, flat spots; skin rough, scaly, scabby; herpes scabby and scurfy; eruptions; whitlow; black pores on nose. Often precedes **Calcarea carb.**

Tartar Emetic.—This is an important remedy in the first stage of influenza; dry cough and affections of the chest; also, in bilious affections; small-pox; asphyxia of new-born infants. Pustular eruptions of the whole body; stupefying headache, with pressure above the eyes; nausea, vomiting and diarrhœa, violent oppression of the stomach; suffocative spasmodic cough; rattling of mucus, coughing and sneezing; difficulty of breathing, especially at night; palpitation of the heart and oppression of the chest.

Thuja.—Headache worse from heating. Eyes: chronic conjunctivitis. Watery, offensive discharge from the ear. Ulcers in the mouth. *Bad effects of vaccination.* Cauliflower excrescences. *Warts.* Bleeding, fungous growths. White, scaly, dry, mealy herpes. Emaciation and deadness of affected parts, Finger-tips numb, as if dead, Extremely fœtid sweat of the feet. Dysuria. Repressed gonorrhœa.

Veratrum Album.—*Cholera,* cholera morbus, with cold sweat on forehead, and cramps; lips bluish; coldness; cramps in the calves of the legs. Gastric catarrh, great weakness, cold, sudden sinking. External chill and coldness with internal heat. Rheumatic fever, with profuse sweat, great weakness and diarrhœa. Typhoid forms of fever in cholera season. Often indicated after **Arsenicum.**

LIST OF REMEDIES PRESCRIBED.

Acidum sulph.,
Aconite,
Apis,
Apocynum cannabinum,
Arnica,
Arsenicum album,
Arsenicum jodatum,
Belladonna,
Calcarea carbonica,
Calendula,
Camphora,
Carbo vegetabilis,
Causticum,
Chamomilla,
China,
Cina,
Colchicum,
Coralium rubrum,
Drosera,
Dulcamara,
Euphrasia,
Gelsemium,
Graphites,

Hepar sulphur,
Ignatia amara,
Ipecac.,
Lachesis,
Mercurius corrosivus,
Mercurius vivus,
Natrum muriaticum,
Nitric acid,
Nux vomica,
Opium,
Podophyllum,
Pulsatilla,
Rhus toxicodendron,
Silicea,
Solanum nig.,
Spongia,
Staphisagria,
Sulphur,
Symphitum,
Tartar emetic,
Thuja,
Veratrum album.

LIST OF DISEASES TREATED IN THIS BOOK, WITH REMEDIES.

The remedies in *italics* are not mentioned in the book where the ailment is treated, but are here suggested as being useful in the disease should the others fail.

Apoplexy.—Aconite, Belladonna, Nux vom., Pulsatilla.

Asthma.—Coral. rub., Spongia, Ipecac., Bryonia.

Bone-wen.—Hepar sulph., Silicea, Nitric acid, Calc. carb., Sulphur.

Black Rot.—Thuja, Nux vom., Podophyllum.

Broken Bones.—Symphitum (*externally*), Hepar sulph.

Bumble Foot.—Calendula (*externally*), Hepar sulph., Silicea.

Chicken-pox.—Arsenicum, Rhus, Belladonna, Silicea.

Chip.—Veratrum, Arsenicum, Aconite, Dulcamara, Colchicum.

Cholera.—Veratrum, Arsenicum, Arsenicum iod., *Camphora*, in first stages. *Carbo veg.*, after exposure to great heat of the sun. *Cuprum*, spasmodic variety. *Podophyllum*, painless cholera morbus.

Constipation.—Nux vom., Bryonia, Opium. *Phosphorus*, inveterate constipation with disappointing calls.

Contusions.—Arnica (*externally*).

6

Consumption (cf. Marasmus).—Hepar sulph., Spongia, Calcarea carb.

Core.—Mercurius viv., Silicea, China.

Coryza—Catarrh.—Mercurius viv., Acidum sulph., Arsenicum, Euphrasia, Dulcamara, Hepar sulph., Gelsemium.

Cough.—Dulcamara, Drosera, Sulphur.

Diarrhœa—Dysentery.—Ipecac., Arsenicum, Chamomilla, Carbo veg., Aconite, Mercurius cor., Nitric acid.

Diseases of the Eye.—Aconite, Euphrasia, Sulphur.

Distemper.—Nux vomica.

Dizziness.—Belladonna, Aconite.

Dropsy.—Apocynum cannab., Apis.

Epilepsy.—Belladonna.

Feathering.—Calcarea carb., Chamomilla, Hepar sulph., Aconite. *Kali phos.*, in "nervous prostration."

Gapes.—Drosera, Dulcamara, Ignatia, Lachesis, China, Cina, Santonine.

Gout.—Bryonia, Rhus tox.

Hernia.—Aconite, Nux vom., Pulsatilla.

Hoarseness.—Aconite, Causticum, Hepar sulph., Pulsatilla.

Humid or Black Disease.—Sulphur.

Indigestion, Dyspepsia.—Nux vom., Pulsatilla, China, Carbo veg.

Itch.—Sulphur, Staphisagria.

Kriebel.—Solanum niger.

Lice.—Sulphur.

Liver Complaint.—Podophyllum. *Chionanthus,* |hypertrophy of liver. *Nux vom.*, in big eaters.

Marasmus (cf. consumption).—Hepar sulph.

Moulting.—Calcarea carb., Natrum mur., Aconite.

Pip.—Spongia, Mercurius viv.

Roup.—Spongia, Hepar sulph., Aconite, Arsenicum, Tartar emetic.

Swelled Crop.—Nux vom., Arsenicum.

Swelled Head.—Belladonna, Bryonia.

Thrush (Aphthæ).—Nitric acid, Mercurius viv., Staphisagria, Thuja.

Tumors, Excrescences.—Arsenicum, Hepar sulph., Thuja.

Vesicles.—Nitric acid.

Warts.—Thuja, Arsenicum, Calcarea carb.,

White Comb.—Sulphur, Staphisagria.

Worms.—Cina, Santonine.

INDEX.

LIST OF

STANDARD HOMŒOPATHIC BOOKS
FOR
DOMESTIC AND VETERINARY PRACTICE.

DOMESTIC PRACTICE.

The Homœopathic Domestic Medicine.–By JOSEPH LAURIE, M.D., L.R.C.S., Edin., etc. Edited and revised with numerous important additions, and the introduction of New Remedies, a Repertory, and a Glossary, by ROBERT J. McCLATCHEY, M.D., Graduate of the Homœopathic Medical College of Pennsylvania, etc. Ninth American Edition. Pp. 1044, octavo. Half Morocco. Boericke & Tafel, Philadelphia. Price, $5.00.

Laurie and McClatchey's great book is the completest work on domestic practice ever published, and is especially adapted to families isolated from all medical attendance, to schools, institutions and communities. Mailed post-paid on receipt of price.

The Homœopathic Domestic Physician.—By CONSTANTINE HERING, M.D. Boericke & Tafel, Philadelphia. Cloth, pp. 458, $2.50.

To Dr. Constantine Hering, the world is indebted for the famous "Homœopathic Domestic Physician," *i.e.*, for the idea of books written by skilled physicians, especially for use in domestic practice. This book is the first of its class ever written, but since it first appeared it has gone through many editions and alterations, and is to-day the favorite book with many intelligent people.

A Guide to Homœopathic Practice.—Designed for the Use of Families and Private Individuals. By J. D. JOHNSON, M.D. Boericke & Tafel, Philadelphia. Pp. 494. Cloth, $2.00.

The distinguishing feature of "Johnson's Guide" is the case with which it is understood by the non-medical. Dr. Johnson is also the author of the well-known work for the medical profession, *Johnson's Therapeutic Key.*

The Stepping-Stone to Homœopathy and Health. By E. H. RUDDOCK, M.D. New American Edition. Edited and Enlarged with the Addition of a Chapter on the Diseases of Women, and one on the *Twelve Tissue Remedies.* By Wm. Boericke, M.D. Boericke & Tafel, Philadelphia. Pp. 256. Cloth, $1.00.

Always a favorite, this book has had new value added to it by Dr. Boericke's work. The chapter on the famous "Twelve Tissue Remedies," of Schüssler is the first attempt to introduce these to the public.

The Text-Book for Domestic Practice; being plain and concise directions for the administration of Homœopathic Medicines in Simple Ailments. By SAMUEL MORGAN, M.D., Physician to the Bath Homœopathic Hospital. Boericke & Tafel, Philadelphia. Pp. 191. 18mo. Cloth. Price, 50 cents.

Dr. Samuel Morgan's *Text-Book for Domestic Practice* is a neat and concise pocket-book containing plain directions for the administiation of "Homœopathic Medicines in Simple Ailments." "By simple ailments," the author, as he says in the Preface, "wants to be understood—those which are, or seem, too trivial to call in medical assistance, and for the relief of which every family practices physic more or less.

VETERINARY WORKS.

A Manual of Homœopathic Veterinary Practice. Boericke & Tafel, Philadelphia. Pp. 684. Half Morocco, $5.00.

The scope of this work is much greater than its title indicates, for it not only gives the treatment for the diseases of *all* domestic animals and fowls, but directions for their care in health, preventive treatment, feeding, training, breeding, etc.

New Manual of Homœopathic Veterinary Medicine. An Easy and Comprehensive Arrangement of Diseases, adapted to the Uses of every Owner of Domestic Animals, Horses, Cattle, Sheep, Swine and Dogs. By J. C. SCHAFFER. Translated from the German by CHARLES J. HEMPEL, M.D. Boericke & Tafel, Philadelphia. Pp. 321, octavo. Price, $2.00.

This standard work on veterinary practice enjoys a wide circulation here and in Germany, and will be found invaluable to the farmer, horse fancier and herdsman.

The Hand-Book to Veterinary Homœopathy. On the Homœopathic Treatment of the Horse, the Ox, the Sheep and the Swine. By JOHN RUSH, Veterinary Surgeon. From the London Edition. Boericke & Tafel, Philadelphia. Pp. 144, 16mo. Cloth. Price, 50 cents.

This is the smallest of our veterinary manuals, and will suit those who dislike to invest at once in a larger and more complete work. Small as it is, however, it will be found to cover most cases of farm practice.

Any of the foregoing books may be had of homœopathic pharmacists, or through the book trade generally.

www.ingramcontent.com/pod-product-compliance
Lightning Source LLC
Chambersburg PA
CBHW031447270326
41930CB00007B/901